OFFICE HUMOR II

by Pete Fagan
and Mark Schaffer

Illustrations by Drew Pallo

Harmony Books/New York

This book is dedicated to our wives, Marjatta Fagan and Sharon Schaffer, who also see the humor in work.

Published by Harmony Books, a division of Crown Publishers, Inc., 201 East 50th Street, New York, New York 10022. Member of the Crown Publishing Group.

Harmony and colophon are trademarks of Crown Publishers, Inc.

Manufactured in the United States of America

Library of Congress Cataloging-in-Publication Data
Fagan, Pete.
    Office humor II / by Pete Fagan and Mark Schaffer ;
illustrations by Drew Pallo. — 1st ed.
        p.   cm.
    Continues: The office humor book.
    1. Office practice—Folklore.   2. Xerography—Folklore.
I. Schaffer, Mark.   II. Pallo, Drew.   III. Title.
GR903.F34   1992
817'.54080355—dc20   91-15543
                                                CIP
ISBN 0-517-58334-8
10 9 8 7 6 5 4 3 2 1

First Edition

Introduction

WORK IS FOR SUCKERS.

Despite the feel-good attitude about work we were fed in the eighties, when business was revered and the workaholic ruled, the office continues to harbor wry-smiling men and women who view their jobs with something less than awe. Nestling in their ergonomically designed cubicles, this army of crafty, unacknowledged satirists pokes fun at the absurdities of the white-collar jungle. Office humor, like graffiti and military humor, is symptomatic of the human instinct to subvert pomposity and let the air out of authority's tires.

As in our first collection, *The Office Humor Book*, there are inspirational lines of workplace philosophy, memos that explain how things *really* get done, healthy cynicism from those who do business with the government, and scads of cartoons celebrating the zaniness of the workplace. We've also gone hi-tech, with fax cover sheets, lots of praise for the marvels of computers (no snickering out there), and, for the first time, we let upper management have their say.

So put these on bulletin boards, post by computers, leave on a coworker's desk, or send one anonymously to your boss. Photocopy, fax, and distribute to the world!

"WHEN I WOKE UP
THIS MORNING
I HAD ONE
NERVE LEFT

AND NOW YOU'RE
GETTING ON IT."

"DID THE BOSS HAVE MUCH TO SAY?"

The sign said,

"SMILE. THINGS COULD
BE WORSE."

So I smiled and sure enough,
things got worse!

FAX COVER SHEET

Date: **Time:**

To:

Company:

Telephone Number: **Fax Number:**

WE HAVE RUN ACROSS SOME ABSOLUTELY IRREFUTABLE STATISTICS THAT SHOW EXACTLY WHY YOU ARE TIRED. AND BROTHER, IT'S NO WONDER YOU'RE TIRED. THERE AREN'T AS MANY PEOPLE ACTUALLY WORKING AS YOU MAY HAVE THOUGHT, AT LEAST NOT ACCORDING TO THE SURVEY RECENTLY COMPLETED.

THE POPULATION OF THIS COUNTRY IS 200 MILLION, 84 MILLION OVER 60 YEARS OF AGE, WHICH LEAVES 116 MILLION TO DO THE WORK. PEOPLE UNDER 16 YEARS OF AGE TOTAL 75 MILLION, WHICH LEAVES 41 MILLION TO DO THE WORK.

THERE ARE 22 MILLION EMPLOYED BY THE GOVERNMENT, WHICH LEAVES 19 MILLION TO DO THE WORK. FOUR MILLION ARE IN THE ARMED FORCES, WHICH LEAVES 15 MILLION TO DO THE WORK. DEDUCT 14,800,000, THE NUMBER IN STATE AND CITY OFFICES, LEAVING 200,000 TO DO THE WORK. THERE ARE 188,000 IN HOSPITALS, INSANE ASYLUMS, ETC., SO THAT LEAVES 12,000 TO DO THE WORK.

NOW IT MAY INTEREST YOU TO KNOW THAT THERE ARE 11,998 PEOPLE IN JAIL, SO THAT LEAVES JUST 2 PEOPLE TO CARRY THE LOAD. THAT'S YOU AND ME - - AND BROTHER I'M GETTING TIRED OF DOING EVERYTHING MYSELF.

TO WHOM IT MAY CONCERN:

    The Occupational Safety and Health Administration (O.S.H.A.) has determined that the maximum safe load capacity on my butt is two persons at one time, unless I install handrails and safety straps.

    As you have arrived sixth in line to ride my ass today, please take a number and wait your turn.

THANK YOU!

YESTERDAY
IS A
MEMORY;

TOMORROW
IS A
VISION;

TODAY
IS A
BITCH!!

**YOU MEAN YOU WANT THE REVISED REVISION
OF THE ORIGINAL REVISED REVISION REVISED?**

"YOU KNOW?
MY BOSS REMINDS ME
OF MY DIAPER.
ALWAYS ON MY ASS,
AND MOST OF THE TIME
FULL OF SHIT!"

ANSWERS PRICE LIST

ANSWERS 75

ANSWERS
(Requiring thought) .   1.25

ANSWERS
(Correct) 2.00

DUMB LOOKS ARE STILL <u>FREE</u>

I try to take just ONE DAY AT A TIME...

...but lately several days have attacked me at once!

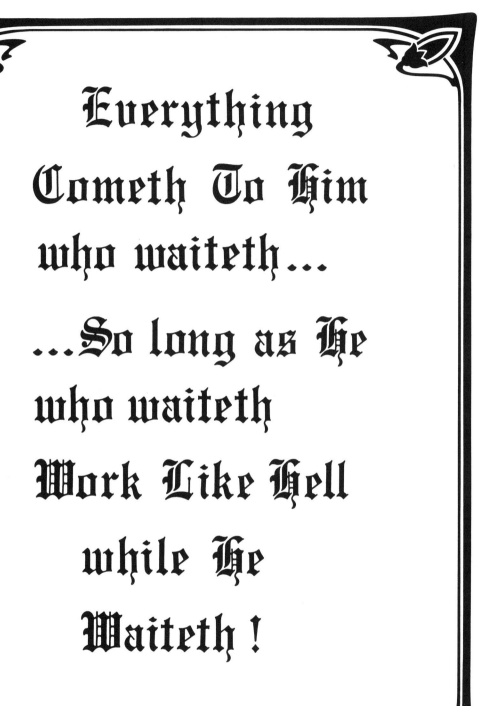

Everything Cometh To Him who waiteth...

...So long as He who waiteth Work Like Hell while He Waiteth !

I am a mushroom.
I must be a mushroom.
They always keep me
in the dark and
feed me bullshit.

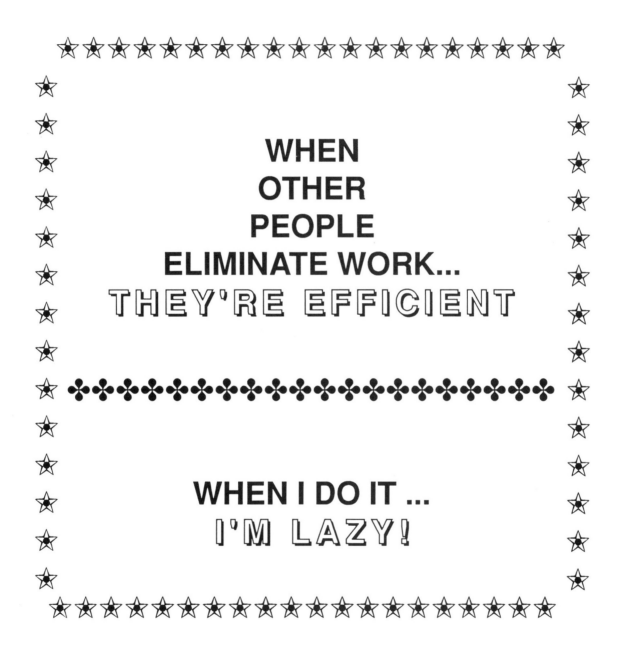

WHEN
OTHER
PEOPLE
ELIMINATE WORK...
THEY'RE EFFICIENT

WHEN I DO IT ...
I'M LAZY!

NO ONE IS COMPLETELY USELESS...

...AT THE VERY LEAST, YOU COULD SERVE AS A BAD EXAMPLE

NOBODY IS PERFECT

Each one of us is a mixture of good qualities and some perhaps not-so-good qualities. In considering our fellow man we should remember his good qualities and realize that his faults only prove that he is, after all, a human being. We should refrain from making harsh judgment of a person just because he happens to be a dirty, rotten, no-good son-of- a- bitch.

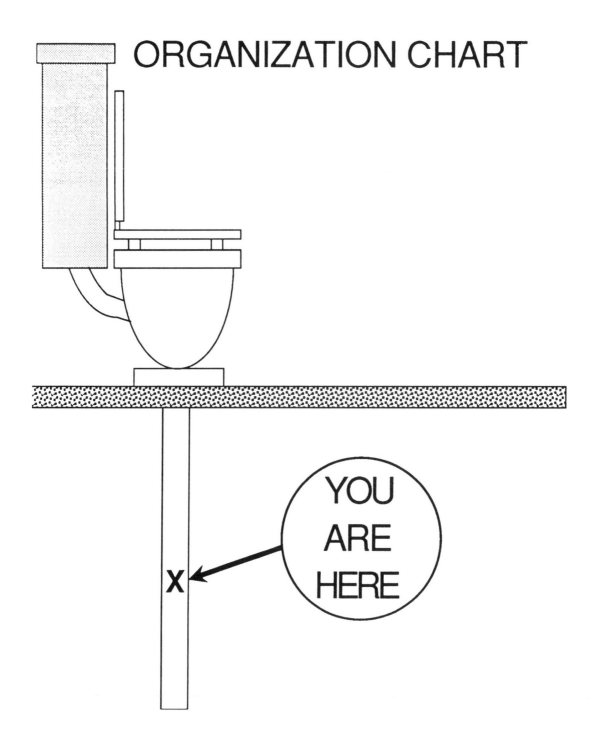

"All progress is based upon a universal innate desire on the part of every organism to live beyond its income."

STRESS

THAT CONFUSION
CREATED WHEN
ONE'S MIND
OVERRIDES THE
BODY'S DESIRE TO
CHOKE THE LIVING
SHIT OUT OF SOME
ASSHOLE WHO
DESPERATELY NEEDS
IT !!

There is <u>never</u> time to do it right

There is <u>always</u> time to do it over.

FAX COVER SHEET

Date: Time:

To:

Company:

Telephone Number: Fax Number:

Thought for the Day

Patience, my ass!
I'm gonna kill somebody!!

A WOMAN
has to do twice as
much as a man to
be considered half
as good.

fortunately, this
isn't difficult.

Oh, that explains the difference in our salaries.

EVOLUTION
OF
AUTHORITY

WHEN GOD
MADE MAN

SHE WAS
ONLY JOKING

HOW TO TELL A BUSINESSMAN
FROM A BUSINESSWOMAN

A businessman is aggressive;
a businesswoman is pushy.

A businessman is good on details;
she's picky.

He loses his temper because he's so involved with his job;
she's bitchy.

When he's depressed (or hung over) everyone tiptoes past his office;
she's moody, so it must be her "time of the month."

He follows through;
she doesn't know when to quit.

He stands firm;
she's hard.

His judgments are *her prejudices.*

He is a man of the world;
she's been around.

He drinks because of the excessive job pressure;
she's a lush.

He isn't afraid to say what he thinks;
she's mouthy.

He exercises authority diligently;
she's power-mad.

He's close-mouthed;
she's secretive.

He's a stern taskmaster;
she's hard to work for.

He climbed the ladder of success;
she slept her way to the top.

GOD, I LOVE THIS PLACE

Please be patient, I only work here because...

...I am too old for a paper route,
...too young for social security,
...and too tired to have an affair.

THE CORPORATE STRUCTURE

CHAIRMAN OF THE BOARD	Leaps tall buildings in a single bound is more powerful than a locomotive is faster than a speeding bullet Walks on Water Gives policy to God
PRESIDENT	Leaps short buildings in a single bound is more powerful than a switch engine is just as fast as a speeding bullet Walks on water if the sea is calm Talks with God
EXECUTIVE VICE PRESIDENT	Leaps short buildings with a running start and favorable winds is almost as powerful as a switch engine is faster than a speeding BB Walks on water in an indoor swimming pool Talks with God if special request is approved
VICE PRESIDENT	Barely clears a Quonset hut Loses tug-of-war with a locomotive Can fire a speeding bullet Swims well is occasionally addressed by God
GENERAL MANAGER	Makes high marks on the wall when trying to leap building Is run over by locomotive Can sometimes handle a gun without inflicting self-injury Dog paddles Talks to animals
MANAGER	Runs into buildings Recognizes locomotive two out of three times Is not issued ammunition Can't stay afloat with a life preserver Talks to walls
TRAINEE	Falls over doorsteps when trying to enter buildings Says "look at the choo choo" Wets himself with a water pistol Plays in mud puddles Mumbles to himself
SECRETARY	Lifts buildings and walks under them Kicks locomotives off the track Catches speeding bullets in her teeth and eats them Freezes water with a single glance SHE IS GOD

GRACE
BEFORE LUNCH

The Lord is my Shepard, I shall not want.
He maketh me lie down and do pushups.
He giveth me Hollywood bread.
He restoreth my waistline.
He leadeth me past the refrigerator for my
    own sake.
He maketh me partake of green beans
    instead of potatoes.
He leadeth me past the pizzeria.
Yea, though I walk through the bakery I shall
    not falter, for Thou art with me.
Thy Tab and Thy Fresca they comfort me.
Thou preparest a diet for me in the presence
    of mine enemies.
Thou anointest my lettuce with lo-cal oil.
My cup will not overflow.
Surely, Granola and Yogurt shall follow me
    all the days of my life.
And I shall live with the pangs of hunger
    forever.

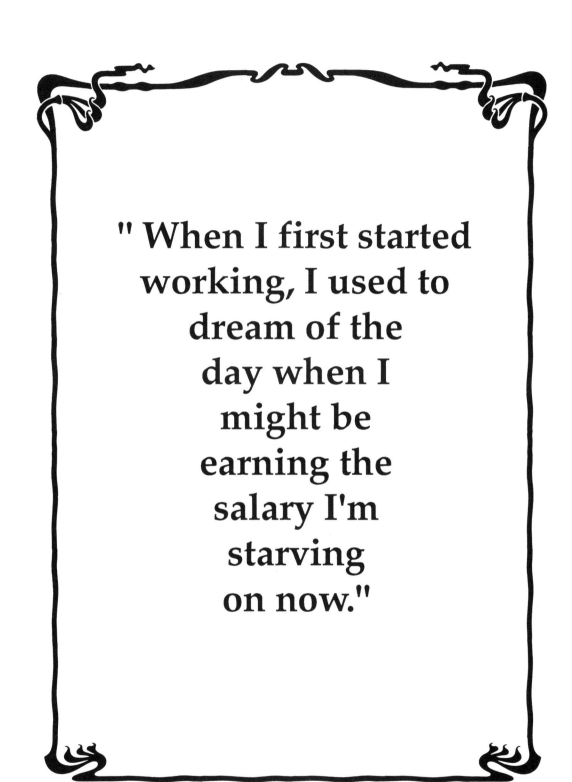

" When I first started
working, I used to
dream of the
day when I
might be
earning the
salary I'm
starving
on now."

TELL ME AGAIN HOW LUCKY I AM TO BE WORKING HERE!!
I KEEP FORGETTING

FAX COVER SHEET

Date: Time:

To:

Company:

Telephone Number: Fax Number:

THESE LAST MINUTE CHANGES
WILL HAVE TO STOP!

THE WORLD'S MOST
WIDELY USED
COMPUTER
LANGUAGE:

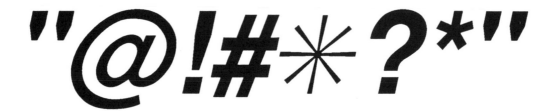

A COMPUTER MAKES AS MANY
MISTAKES IN TWO MINUTES AS
TWENTY PEOPLE MAKE IN TWENTY
YEARS.

If builders built buildings the way
programmers write programs, then
the first woodpecker that came along
would destroy civilization.

This Office Has Not
Recorded A
Computer
Related Accident In

27

DAYS

It Has Not
Recorded A
Computer
Related Death In

53

DAYS

Keep Up The Good Work Everyone!

ARGUING WITH A
COMPUTER
PROGRAMMER
IS LIKE WRESTLING
WITH A PIG;
EVERYONE GETS DIRTY
BUT THE
PROGRAMMER
LOVES IT.

WARNING

THIS MACHINE IS SUBJECT TO BREAKDOWNS DURING PERIODS OF CRITICAL NEED!!

A SPECIAL CIRCUIT IN THE MACHINE CALLED A CRISIS DETECTOR SENSES THE OPERATOR'S EMOTIONAL STATE IN TERMS OF HOW DESPERATELY HE OR SHE NEEDS TO USE THE MACHINE.

THE CRISIS DETECTOR THEN CREATES A MALFUNCTION PROPORTIONAL TO THE DESPERATION OF THE OPERATOR. THREATENING THE MACHINE WITH VIOLENCE ONLY AGGRAVATES THE SITUATION.

LIKEWISE, ATTEMPTS TO USE ANY OTHER MACHINE MAY CAUSE IT TO MALFUNCTION ALSO. THEY BELONG TO THE SAME UNION.

JUST KEEP YOUR COOL AND SAY NICE THINGS TO THE MACHINE.

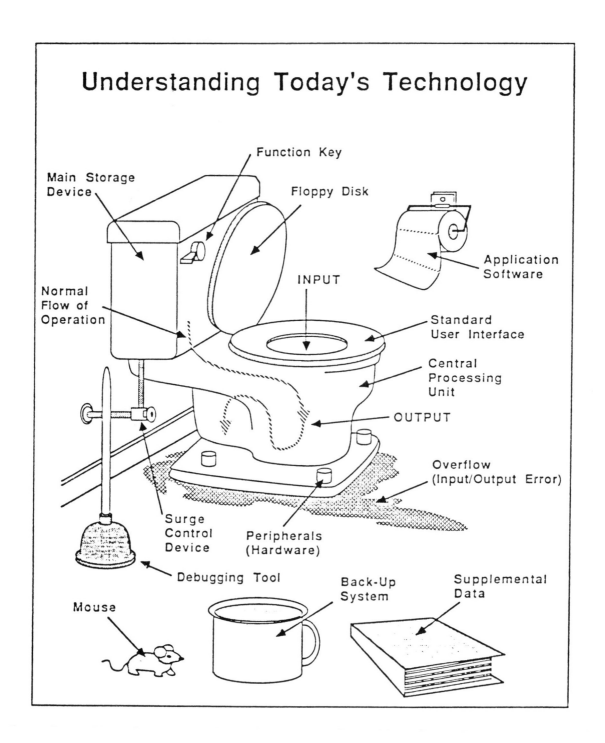

FAX COVER SHEET

Date: **Time:**

To:

Company:

Telephone Number: **Fax Number:**

DON'T RUSH ME:

I'M MAKING MISTAKES

AS FAST AS I CAN.

OFFICIAL NOTICE

THE
BEATINGS
WILL
CONTINUE
UNTIL
MORALE
IMPROVES

THE
MANAGEMENT

"Of course I want it today!
If I wanted it tomorrow
I'd give it to you <u>tomorrow!</u>"

SUBJ: MANAGEMENT BY IMPEDIMENT

1. <u>Scope</u>. This program applies to all offices.

2. <u>Background</u>. There exists a growing concern in the central office that a substantial number of programs are not as functionally vital as desired. After extensive research, it has been established that the problem stems from an inadequate appreciation of the principles of Darwinian Sociology. It is the position of management that only through overcoming obstacles can any entity improve itself.

3. <u>Implementation</u>. In the future, all managers will proceed to place obstacles in the path of their proposed programs. If any program seems to be progressing too rapidly, a suggested solution is to utilize the "zero-funding" ploy. If repeated doses of "zero-funding" show no major weaknesses, then drastic measures may be required. Removal of certain personnel and reorganization is suggested.

It is essential for all managers to realize that while benign neglect may suffice in the early stages of development, active malevolence may be required as the system approaches completion. Only through constant application of the principles of MANAGEMENT BY IMPEDIMENT can we ensure that only the most vigorous and vital programs survive.

<u>THE MANAGEMENT</u>

NOTICE!

YOU ARE REQUESTED TO TAKE

A BATH

BEFORE REPORTING TO WORK

Since we have to kiss your ass to get you to do anything, we want it clean.

the Management

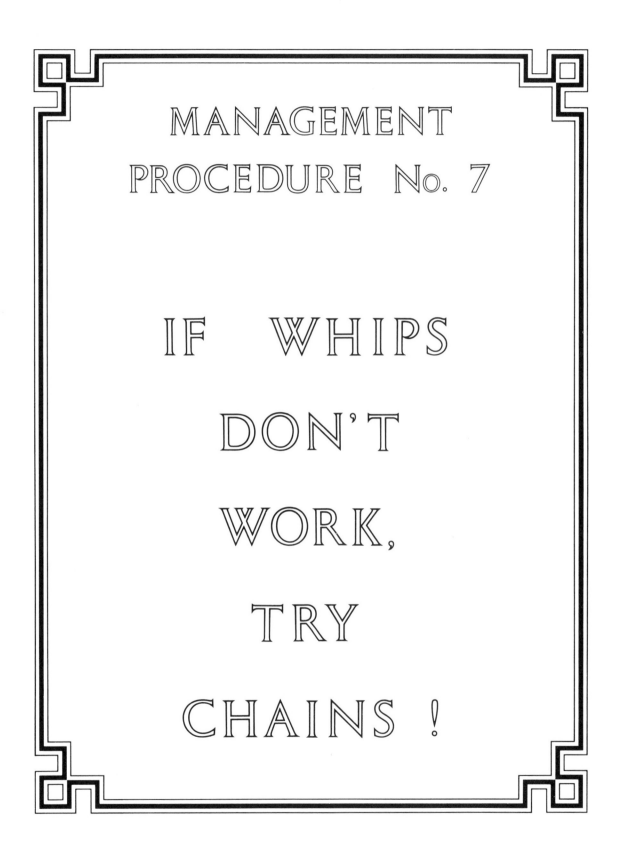

MANAGEMENT
PROCEDURE No. 7

IF WHIPS
DON'T
WORK,
TRY
CHAINS !

NOTICE
TO ALL EMPLOYEES
SIGN UP FOR ADDITIONAL TRAINING

It is now and always has been the policy of this company to assure its employees that they are well trained. Through our Special High Intensity Training (SHIT) Program, we have given our employees more SHIT than any other company in the area.

If any employee feels that he or she does not receive enough SHIT on this job, or that he or she could advance to another position by taking more SHIT, see your immediate supervisor.

Our Management people are specially trained to assure you that you will get all the SHIT you can stand.

Personnel Department

Please sign on the dotted line to get your name on the Management's SHIT list.

IF YOU CAME HERE
TO BITCH
YOU HAVE ALREADY USED UP
98% OF YOUR TIME

I WOULD LIKE TO SUGGEST THAT
YOU USE THE REMAINING 2%
TO FIND THE DOOR

Yea, though I walk
through the valley
of the shadow of death
I shall fear no evil.
Cause I am the meanest
"Son of a Bitch"
in the valley.

✱✱✱✱✱✱✱✱✱✱✱✱✱✱✱✱✱✱✱✱✱✱✱✱✱✱✱✱✱

ENGAGE
BRAIN
BEFORE
STARTING
TONGUE

✱✱✱✱✱✱✱✱✱✱✱✱✱✱✱✱✱✱✱✱✱✱✱✱✱✱✱✱✱

NOTICE

THIS OFFICE REQUIRES NO PHYSICAL
FITNESS PROGRAM – EVERYONE
GETS PLENTY OF EXERCISE JUMPING
TO CONCLUSIONS, FLYING OFF THE
HANDLE, RUNNING DOWN THE BOSS,
KNIFING FRIENDS IN THE BACK,
DODGING RESPONSIBILITY,
POLISHING THE APPLE AND
PUSHING THEIR LUCK.

THE CREATION

In the Beginning was THE PLAN
And with it came the Procedures

And the Procedures were without form
And THE PLAN was completely without substance

And the darkness was on the face of the Workers
And they spake unto their supervisors, saying:
"It is a crock of shit and it stinkith."

And the Supervisors went to their Project Leaders
And sayeth:
"It is a pail of dung, and none may abide the odor thereof"

And the Project Leaders went unto their Department Managers
and sayeth unto them:
"It is a container of excrement, and it is very strong,
such that none here may abide by it."

And the Department Managers went unto their Division Director
and sayeth unto him:
" It is a vessel of fertilizer, and none may abide its strength."

And the Division Director went unto the Executive Vice President,
and sayeth unto her:
"It contains that which aids plant growth, and is very strong."

And the Executive Vice President went unto the President,
and sayeth unto him:
"It promoteth growth, and is very powerful."

And the President went unto the Board of Directors,
and sayeth unto them:
"This powerful new plan will actively promote the growth and efficiency of the
Corporation".

And the Board of Directors looked upon THE PLAN,
and saw that it was good,
And THE PLAN became the POLICY

BEFORE YOU GIVE ME
A PIECE OF
YOUR MIND...

...ARE YOU SURE
YOU CAN
AFFORD IT?

Turnabout Is
Fair Play

Ever since this company was founded, employees have been inadvertently taking pens, rulers, paper, paper clips and rubber bands, as well as all sorts of other supplies, home with them. Once there, they forget to bring them back. That's certainly understandable. And no one can blame family members for using those items; after all, we don't have our name printed on them.

While the situation poses problems for our supply people, owing to the erratic ordering required to properly supply our employees with the necessary operating tools, those problems have been relatively minor.

Still many employees no doubt feel as though they have somehow cheated the company, and to be truthful, these "lost" supplies have cost us thousands of dollars every year. So, to ease everyone's conscience, and in the spirit of fairness, beginning Tuesday, all employees will bring paper, typewriter ribbons, and all other supplies from home for use here. Let's see how that works for a few years.

FAX COVER SHEET

Date: Time:

To:

Company:

Telephone Number: Fax Number:

what part of

NO

don't you understand?

AN ELEPHANT IS A MOUSE
BUILT TO
GOVERNMENT SPECIFICATIONS

MOTTO
OF ALL GOVERNMENT BUREAUCRATS

"ANYTHING WORTH DOING ISN'T WORTH DOING...YET!"

FOR THOSE WHO HAVE TO DEAL WITH THE FEDERAL GOVERNMENT:

Department of Administration
Bureau of Agency Services
Office of the Board of Commissions
Washington, D.C.

WORK DEFINITIONS

CONTRACTOR - A gambler who never gets to shuffle, cut or deal.

BID OPENING - A poker game in which the losing hand wins.

BID - A wild guess carried out to two decimal places.

LOW BIDDER - A contractor who is wondering what he left out.

ENGINEER'S ESTIMATE - The cost of construction in heaven.

PROJECT MANAGER - The conductor of an orchestra in which every musician is in a different union.

CRITICAL PATH METHOD - A management technique for losing your shirt under perfect control.

DELAYED PAYMENT - A tourniquet applied to the pockets.

COMPLETION DATE - The point at which liquidated damages begin.

LIQUIDATED DAMAGES - A penalty for failing to achieve the impossible.

AUDITOR - People who go in after the war is lost and bayonet the wounded.

LAWYER - People who go in after the auditors and strip the bodies.

TEST YOUR PENTAGON IQ

CAN YOU MATCH EACH OFFICIAL DEFENSE DEPARTMENT TERM WITH ITS CORRECT DEFINITION?

1 Circadian Deregulation   a PROPAGANDA

2 Alternative Hostility   b COMBAT

3 Dynamic Processing Environment   c PEACE

4 Enmity Stimulation   d NUCLEAR WAR

5 Violence Processing   e DEATH

6 Violence Source   f WEAPON

7 Permanent Prehostility   g KILL ZONE

Answers: 1-e, 2-d, 3-g, 4-a, 5-b, 6-f and 7-c

INTERNATIONAL SYMBOLS

IN ITS EFFORT TO STANDARDIZE HIGHWAY SIGNS AND MAKE THEM CONFORM TO THE EUROPEAN SYSTEM, THE FEDERAL GOVERNMENT HAS BEEN REPLACING WORD WITH SYMBOLS. BELOW ARE MOST RECENT EXAMPLES APPROVED BY UNESCO, AS PART OF THE WORLDWIDE IDENTIFICATION CODE, ALONG WITH THE MEANING OF EACH SYMBOL. SOON TO BE APPEARING ROADSIDE:

1. Village made entirely from soap. 5 kilometers.

2. Do not throw cashews from your car.

3. Bears playing cellos, next 10 kilometers.

4. Turnips have been planted roadside for your convenience.

5. The local taffy has been condemned.

6. Although not expressly forbidden, the playing of tubas annoys the bear.

7. There are funny things in the shrubs.

8. It is forbidden to pummel the ravens with pillows.

9. Clown crossing next 5 kilometers.

10. In stormy weather, pocketbooks may be struck by lightning.

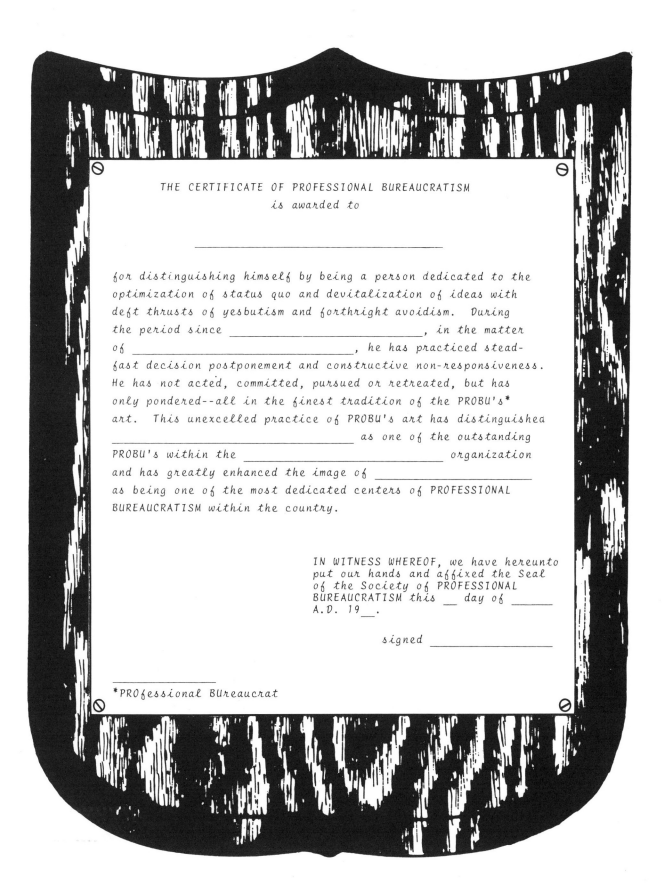

THE CERTIFICATE OF PROFESSIONAL BUREAUCRATISM
is awarded to

_____

for distinguishing himself by being a person dedicated to the
optimization of status quo and devitalization of ideas with
deft thrusts of yesbutism and forthright avoidism. During
the period since _____, in the matter
of _____, he has practiced stead-
fast decision postponement and constructive non-responsiveness.
He has not acted, committed, pursued or retreated, but has
only pondered--all in the finest tradition of the PROBU's*
art. This unexcelled practice of PROBU's art has distinguished
_____ as one of the outstanding
PROBU's within the _____ organization
and has greatly enhanced the image of _____
as being one of the most dedicated centers of PROFESSIONAL
BUREAUCRATISM within the country.

IN WITNESS WHEREOF, we have hereunto
put our hands and affixed the Seal
of the Society of PROFESSIONAL
BUREAUCRATISM this __ day of _____
A.D. 19__.

signed _____

_____
*PROfessional BUreaucrat

THE COWBOY AFTER O.S.H.A.

Here's a Cowboy after the Office of Safety and Health Administration gets ahold of him.

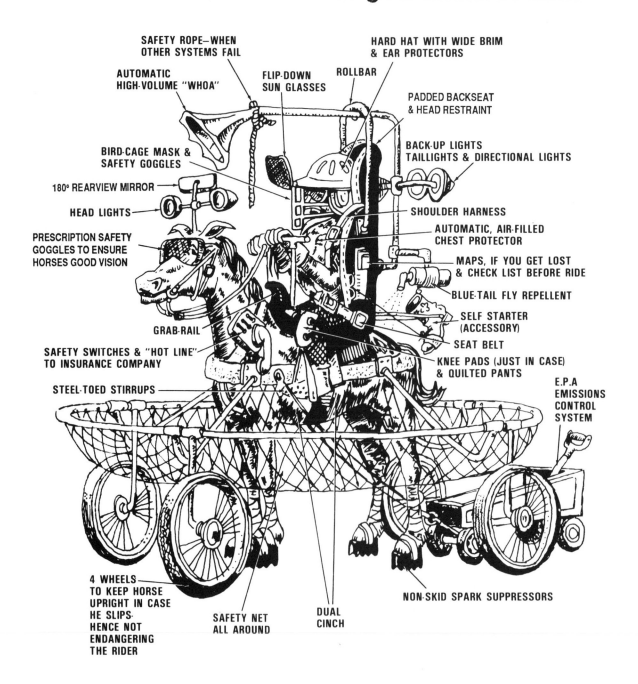

SAFETY ROPE—WHEN OTHER SYSTEMS FAIL

AUTOMATIC HIGH-VOLUME "WHOA"

FLIP-DOWN SUN GLASSES

ROLLBAR

HARD HAT WITH WIDE BRIM & EAR PROTECTORS

PADDED BACKSEAT & HEAD RESTRAINT

BIRD-CAGE MASK & SAFETY GOGGLES

BACK-UP LIGHTS TAILLIGHTS & DIRECTIONAL LIGHTS

180° REARVIEW MIRROR

HEAD LIGHTS

SHOULDER HARNESS

AUTOMATIC, AIR-FILLED CHEST PROTECTOR

PRESCRIPTION SAFETY GOGGLES TO ENSURE HORSES GOOD VISION

MAPS, IF YOU GET LOST & CHECK LIST BEFORE RIDE

BLUE-TAIL FLY REPELLENT

SELF STARTER (ACCESSORY)

GRAB-RAIL

SEAT BELT

SAFETY SWITCHES & "HOT LINE" TO INSURANCE COMPANY

KNEE PADS (JUST IN CASE) & QUILTED PANTS

STEEL-TOED STIRRUPS

E.P.A EMISSIONS CONTROL SYSTEM

4 WHEELS TO KEEP HORSE UPRIGHT IN CASE HE SLIPS- HENCE NOT ENDANGERING THE RIDER

SAFETY NET ALL AROUND

DUAL CINCH

NON-SKID SPARK SUPPRESSORS

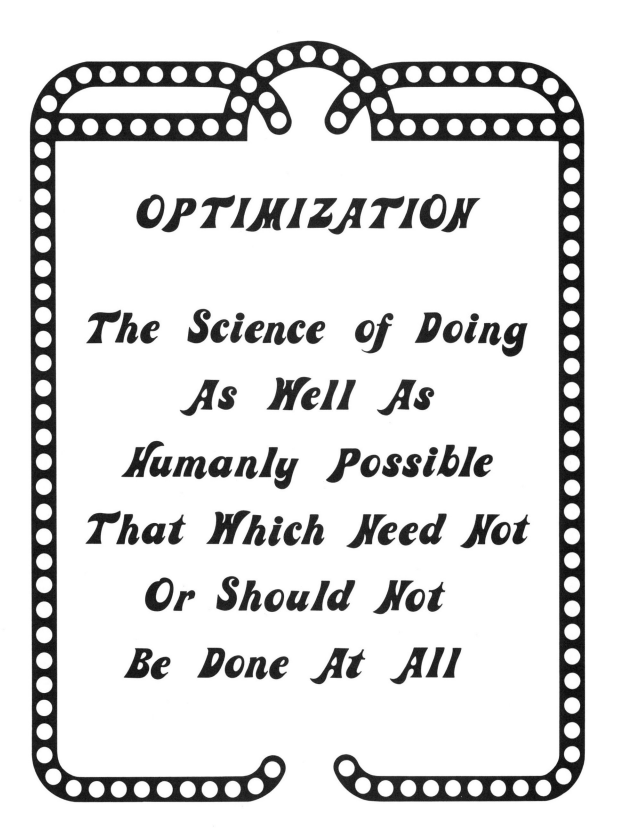

OPTIMIZATION

The Science of Doing
As Well As
Humanly Possible
That Which Need Not
Or Should Not
Be Done At All

RESEARCH DEFINITIONS

It has long been known -
I haven't bothered to look up the original reference.

Of great theoretical and practical importance -
Interesting to me.

While it has not been possible to provide answers to these questions -
The experiment didn't work, but I figured I could get some publicity out of it.

Handled with extreme care during experiment -
Not dropped.

Typical results are shown -
The best results are shown.

Presumably at longer times -
I didn't take the time to find out.

It is believed that -
I think.

It is generally believed that -
A couple of other folks think so too.

It might be argued that -
I have such a good answer for this objection that I shall now raise it.

It is clear that much additional information will be required before a complete understanding -
I don't understand it.

Correct within an order of magnitude -
Wrong.

**my work
is so secret...**

**...I don't even
know what
I'm doing!**

FAX COVER SHEET

Date: Time:

To:

Company:

Telephone Number: Fax Number:

Strong letter will follow

WHOSE JOB IS IT?

THIS IS A STORY ABOUT FOUR PEOPLE NAMED EVERYBODY, SOMEBODY, ANYBODY AND NOBODY. THERE WAS AN IMPORTANT JOB TO BE DONE AND EVERYBODY WAS SURE THAT SOMEBODY WOULD DO IT.

ANYBODY COULD HAVE DONE IT, BUT NOBODY DID IT. SOMEBODY GOT ANGRY ABOUT THAT BECAUSE IT WAS EVERYBODY'S JOB.

EVERYBODY THOUGHT ANYBODY COULD DO IT, BUT NOBODY REALIZED THAT EVERYBODY WOULDN'T DO IT.

IT ENDED UP THAT EVERYBODY BLAMED SOMEBODY WHEN NOBODY DID WHAT ANYBODY COULD HAVE DONE.

When someone you greatly admire and respect appears to be thinking deep thoughts, they probably are thinking about lunch.

WORK RULES:

1. **KEEP** YOUR EYE ON THE BALL

2. **KEEP** YOUR SHOULDER TO THE WHEEL

3. **KEEP** YOUR NOSE TO THE GRINDSTONE

Now try to work in that position!

CERTIFICATE

For Your Very Outstanding Performance

"ONE ATTABOY"

One thousand "Attaboys" qualifies you to be a leader of men, work overtime with a smile, explain assorted problems to management, and be looked upon as a local hero, without a raise in pay. NOTE: One "Awshit" wipes the board clean and you have to start all over again.

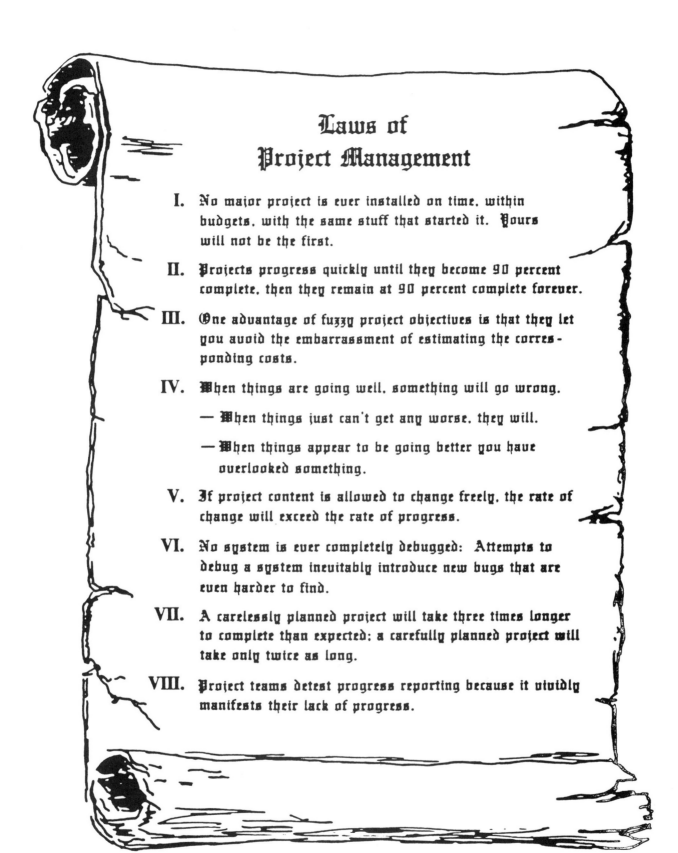

Laws of Project Management

I. No major project is ever installed on time, within budgets, with the same stuff that started it. Yours will not be the first.

II. Projects progress quickly until they become 90 percent complete, then they remain at 90 percent complete forever.

III. One advantage of fuzzy project objectives is that they let you avoid the embarrassment of estimating the corresponding costs.

IV. When things are going well, something will go wrong.

— When things just can't get any worse, they will.

— When things appear to be going better you have overlooked something.

V. If project content is allowed to change freely, the rate of change will exceed the rate of progress.

VI. No system is ever completely debugged: Attempts to debug a system inevitably introduce new bugs that are even harder to find.

VII. A carelessly planned project will take three times longer to complete than expected; a carefully planned project will take only twice as long.

VIII. Project teams detest progress reporting because it vividly manifests their lack of progress.

PROPER
PLANNING
PREVENTS
PISS
POOR
PERFORMANCE

OFFICE HUMOR II

Everyone brings us happiness.

Some by arriving.

Some by leaving.

Successful Purchasing . . .

. . . is being graceful enough to take tickets

off the hands of a vendor

you know you'll never do business with.

To _____

Date _____ Time _____

WHILE YOU WERE GOOFING OFF...

M _____

of _____

Phone _____
      Area Code   **Number**   **Extension**

☐ Phoned to harrass you   ☐ Wants you to return call:

☐ Stopped by to harrass you   ☐ Eventually

☐ Didn't sound important   ☐ Immediately

☐ Sounded ridiculously important   ☐ Yesterday

☐ Message was: _____

_____

_____

_____

☐ I forgot the message

☐ Initials of message bungler: _____

Certificate of Upgrade to Complete Asshole

is Awarded to

*In Recognition of Your Obnoxious Attitude, Ability to Piss People Off,
Complete Asinine Juvenile Behavior and Total Dedication to Personal Gain
Without Regard to the Many Hardships You Have Forced Upon Friends, Family and
Others During Your Lifetime, You Have Become a
Legend in YOUR Own Mind.*

*To Recognize Your Upgrade From Half-assed to Complete Asshole,
Gives All Concerned Great Satisfaction.
If Anyone for Any Reason Doubts Your Status,*

JUST BE YOURSELF!

_____   _____
Date   Signed

THE COPIER
IS OUT OF ORDER

NO	- We cannot fix it
YES	- We have called the service man
YES	- He will be in today
NO	- We do not know how long it will take
NO	- We do not know what caused it
NO	- We do not know who broke it
YES	- We are keeping it
NO	- We do not know what you are going to do
YES	- We know what to do with it

OFFICE HOURS

Open most days about 9 or 10,
occasionally as early as 7, but
some days as late as 12 or 1.

We close about 5:30 or 6, occasionally about 4 or 5, but
sometimes as late as 11 or 12.

Some days or afternoons, we
aren't here at all, and lately
I've been here just about all
the time, except when I'm
someplace else, but I should be
here then too.

OFFICE HUMOR II

WORK
IS
A
GOOD
PLACE
TO
HIDE

FAX COVER SHEET

Date: *Time:*

To:

Company:

Telephone Number: *Fax Number:*

IF YOUR CHECK IS IN THE MAIL
PLEASE DISREGARD THIS REMINDER.

Dear Earthling,
Hi!
I am a creature from outer space.
I have transformed myself into
this piece of paper.
Right now, I am having sex with
your fingers.
I know you like it because you are
smiling.
Please pass me on to someone else
because I'm really horny.
Thanks!

SHIT HAPPENS

(As Interpreted By Various Religions)

TAOISM........Shit Happens.

CONFUCIANISM..Confucius Say, "Shit Happens."

BUDDHISM....If Shit Happens, It Really Isn't Shit.

ZEN BUDDHISM..What Is The SOUND of
                                        Shit Happening?

HINDUISM.....This Shit Happened Before!

ISLAM........If Shit Happens,
                                It Is The Will Of Allah.

PROTESTANTISM..Let Shit Happen
                                        To Somebody Else.

CATHOLICISM..If Shit Happens, You Deserve It.

JUDAISM.....Why Does Shit Always
                                Happen To Us?

THE SMOKER'S PRAYER

Heavenly Father, hear my plea
And grant my lungs serenity!

Give me strength to kick the smoking
That's been causing all my choking.

Let my breath be fresh and clean,
Without a trace of nicotine.

Guide me by your holy means,
Past all cigarette machines.

I ask your help,
    And it's no wonder
If I don't quit,
    I'm 6 feet under!!
                Amen

I SMOKE!

THANK YOU
FOR NOT
BITCHING

PARKING VIOLATION

---------   ------------------
STATE   LICENSE NUMBER

---------   ------------------
TIME   MAKE OF AUTOMOBILE

This is not a ticket, but if it were within my power, you would receive two. Because of your bull-headed, inconsiderate, feeble attempt at parking, you have taken enough room for a 20 mule team, 3 Amtraks, 4 747's, 5 BMW's and an eighteen wheeler. The reason for giving you this is so that in the future you may think of someone else other than yourself. Besides I don't like domineering, egotistical or simple minded drivers and you probably fit into one of these categories.

I sign off wishing you an early transmission failure (on the expressway at about 4:30 pm). Also may the fleas of a thousand camels infest your armpits.

CHILDREN
Tired of being
Harrassed by your
Stupid Parents?

ACT NOW!
Move Out, Get a Job
Pay Your Own Bills,
While You Still
Know Everything.

WANTED:
GOOD WOMAN

**Must Be Able To
Clean, Cook, Sew,
Dig Worms And
Clean Fish.**

**Must Have Own Boat
With Motor.**

**Please Send Picture
Of Boat And Motor.**

THE TEN COMMANDMENTS
OF GOOD BUSINESS WRITING

I Each pronoun should agree with their antecedent.

II Just between you and I, case is important.

III A preposition is a poor word to end a sentence with.

IV Verbs has to agree with their subjects.

V Don't use no double negatives.

VI A writer musn't shift your point of view.

VII When dangling, don't use participles.

VIII Join clauses good, like a conjunction should.

IX Don't write a run-on sentence because it is difficult when you got to puncuate it so it makes sense when the reader reads what you wrote.

X About sentence fragments.

PLEASE STAND BY

I'M EXPERIENCING
A TEMPORARY LOSS
OF MOTIVATION

I HAVE DEVELOPED AN ATTITUDE!